# Focus on

## William Blake's *Songs of Innocence and of Experience*

Matt Simpson

GREENWICH EXCHANGE
LONDON

**Greenwich Exchange, London**

Focus on
William Blake's
*Songs of Innocence and of Experience*
©Matt Simpson 2008

First published in Great Britain in 2008
All rights reserved

Printed and bound by Q3 Digital/Litho, Loughborough
Tel: 01509 213456
Typesetting and layout by Jude Keen, London
Tel: 020 8355 4541
Cover design by December Publications, Belfast
Tel: 028 90286559

Greenwich Exchange Website: www.greenex.co.uk

Cataloguing in Publication Data is available from the
British Library

ISBN-13: 978-1-906075-26-2

*A good song, even if set to no music and read in silence, still sings and dances in the reader's brain.*

H. J. C. Grierson

*The true Blakean feels that to explain a single line of Blake he must somehow explain all of him, and in at least one sense he is correct.*

Hazard Adams

*Poetry admits not a letter that is Insignificant.*

William Blake

*for Peter Street*

I would like to express my gratitude to Monika and Angela for bearing with me, to Nevil who listened too and who knows his Bible much better than I do, to John Farrell for his encouragement and, as always, to my good friend and best critic, Professor John Lucas, who read the typescript and offered many invaluable comments.

# Contents

# Introduction

Poems arranged in sequences can converse with one another, agree or argue, echo or elucidate what others are saying; they can feed into one another, with the result that the whole becomes greater than the sum of its parts. In other words they exist in a context that is dynamic and intimate. Blake intended his *Songs of Innocence and of Experience* to work in this way when he set up a living relationship between *Innocence* and *Experience*, declaring them to show "the Two Contrary States of the Human Soul". "Without Contraries", he famously said in *The Marriage of Heaven and Hell,* "is no Progression. Attraction and Repulsion, Reason and Energy, Love and Hate are necessary to Human existence." This is not a simple matter of dualistic either–or thinking. Blake's Contraries are inseparable parts of one equation. It is not a matter of either–or but of either-*and*-or. In a word, what Blake offers is something holistic. It is better to think in terms of a spectrum or to see Innocence and Experience as a kind of sliding scale, one which measures the degree of Innocence and Experience each of us can lay claim to. As Peter Ackroyd says in his biography of the poet, the poems work "together to form a complete and coherent statement".[1] I would have to argue with the somewhat cold word 'statement' and replace it with the more alive 'experience', recalling in doing so the American poet Dana Gioia's "one does not experience poetry – or any art – solely through the intellect but with the whole of one's humanity."[2]

Almost everyone, in a kind of folk-memory way, knows at least one or two of the poems. They remember them from school or from having read them in anthologies. They usually include *The Tyger, The Lamb, The Sick Rose,* and *London.* Fine poems as they are in their own right, it is nevertheless important to know they have been extracted – one might say

1

dislocated – from what is in effect an artfully arranged set of forty-six poems – nineteen in *Songs of Innocence* and twenty-seven (if we include *A Divine Image*) in *Songs of Experience.* Given what has been said above, it's possible that a number of readers deny themselves access to the dynamism of the sequence. Even those who have read the poems as a set may have simply read them in black print on white pages. This means the stunning pictorial context Blake gave them is missed. The result therefore is that the poems are not always read in the way their author intended, in what I have called elsewhere a three-dimensional way.[3] Finding Blake's illustrations later can be startling and may in some cases even be at odds with the way the poems have been previously looked at and thought about. And there is a further dimension – one lost to all of us. It is known that Blake composed musical settings for them. Martin K. Nurmi tells us that Blake's

> composition of poetry during the early period was accompanied, evidently, by musical composition in the form of melodies to which he is said to have sung his songs – which as a contemporary J. T. Smith said were "sometimes most singularly beautiful and were noted down by musical professors". Whether he actually composed music for all of his songs simultaneously with writing the words, as an early biographical sketch ... suggests, his lyrics are singable, as shown by the very large number of musical settings of them by contemporary composers.[4]

(By 'contemporary' Nurmi means composers like Vaughan Williams, Benjamin Britten, Virgil Thomson, William Bolcom, among the many who have set Blake's poems to music).[5] What wouldn't we give to make discovery of those professors' noting-downs!

Influenced in his art by medieval illuminated manuscripts and in music and poetry by the ancient harp-accompanied prophets and bards as well as by hymns, nursery rhymes and popular ballads, Blake was reinventing multi-media presentation of poetry. He was also determinedly, as a politically committed poet, writing within a popular tradition as against what we might simply call 'polite literature' – a tradition that was and has continued to be a living tradition in radical working-class circles.

*Songs of Innocence* was first published in book form as a set of hand-coloured engravings in 1789, of which twenty-one copies survive. The poems in this collection were then rebound to incorporate *Songs of Experience* (first advertised in 1793) to become *Songs of Innocence and of Experience* published in 1794, of which twenty-seven copies survive. There is no separate *Songs of Experience* – Blake was almost certainly afraid of being arrested for writing and publishing seditious material. Of the surviving copies of the combined work none follows a conventional order: the combination of poems is never quite the same and some poems in certain copies are excluded. Certain poems from the satire called *An Island in the Moon*, written in 1784 when Blake was twenty-seven, were included. Some from *Innocence* were transferred to *Experience*. For the purposes of this study, I am using the Oxford edition published first in 1967 by the Trianon Press with an introduction and commentary by Geoffrey Keynes. This reproduces Blake's engravings in full colour and in the same size as his originals; it also prints the text of poems on the verso of each plate. I have for the most part retained Blake's spelling and punctuation. In the process of listening in to what these poems are saying to one another and to the world, I have inevitably been obliged to find different ways of recording the same observations.

Writing about *Songs of Innocence and of Experience* has its problems. The poems exist in their own right, perfectly say themselves, and in an ideal world would need no commentary. The ideal reader would be one involved in a cumulatively dynamic experience, sensitive to every possible nuance. Poems,

3

as the American poet Robert Lowell insisted, are "events and not records of events" – which is a way of saying that the words poems are made of are alive with energy and require more than the intellect for their appreciation. As he himself said in his *Proverbs of Hell,* "What is now proved was once only imagined" – the word "only" being heavily ironic. Imagination to Blake was sacred and Reason its deadly opposite.

But we don't live in an ideal world. And if we do take poems apart we must remember to put them back again in the hope that exegesis has been able to demonstrate what is palpably and valuably *there* and hopefully to lead to fresh and deeper ways of appreciating. E. P. Thompson talks wisely of "that universe of Blakean symbolism in which we must turn from one poem to another for cumulative elucidation". He goes on to warn us:

> There was ... an incandescence in his art in which incompatible traditions met – tried to marry – argued as contraries – were held in a polarised tension. If one may be wrong to look for a coherent system, there are certainly constellations of related attitudes and images – connected insights – but the moment when we attempt a rational exegesis we are imposing bounds on these insights.[6]

It goes without saying that the primary key to Blake's universe is the Bible. The quotations given in this commentary are taken from the Authorized (King James) Version, the one Blake and his contemporaries intimately knew.

**Notes**
[1] Peter Ackroyd, *Blake* (Sinclair Stevenson, 1995).
[2] Dana Gioia, *Introducton* to his translation of Montale's *Mottetti* (Greywolf Press, 1990).
[3] Matt Simpson, 'Blake's *Songs of Innocence and Experience*' in *William Blake,* edited and introduced by John Lucas (Longman Critical Readers, 1998).

[4] Martin K. Nurmi, *William Blake* (Hutchinson, 1975).

[5] An account of these may be found in Donald Fitch's *Blake Set to Music* (University of California Press, 1990).

[6] E. P. Thompson, *Witness Against the Beast: William Blake and the Moral Law* (Cambridge University Press, 1993).

# 1. Piper sit thee down and write: *Songs of Innocence*

## *Introduction*

We cannot know for certain whether, in the process of writing *Songs of Innocence*, Blake already had *Songs of Experience* in mind. There are commentators who posit a critical moment in Blake's private life (the temptation in *My Pretty Rose Tree*) or a growing realisation of the social conditions around him or of events on the political stage (the American War of Independence beginning in 1775 and the French Revolution in 1789) and awareness of the growing power of censorship, some or all of which made him see things differently. Though we know these matters were of a profound importance to him, it is, however, highly unlikely he had a sudden conversion to a 'more realistic' view of life. Blake was not a realist; he was a visionary. What is important to recognise is that Innocence is a condition of soul belonging to Eternity which has its progressively constrained being in the world of Experience. The world of Experience, as we shall see, is implicit in *Songs of Innocence*.

*Songs of Innocence* is not just a sequence of poems for children; its appeal is to whatever there is of the child in us: it measures the degree of Innocence we can lay claim to. Books of verse for children were popular at this time. They were mostly didactic and pietistic. Ackroyd insists:

> there can be no doubt that Blake was trying to capitalise on the growing market for such literature in his period ... He was trying to use a conventional and marketable form for his own purposes.'[1]

Blake had to make a living; he was an artisan, not an ivory-tower poet: but he was also a man with a mission. Whereas conventional verses for children, in the guise of religion (which he considered false and hypocritical), promoted the constraints of virtuous living and good behaviour, Blake, sometimes giving the child its own voice, offered, as he knew the Bible did, reassurances of spiritual freedom As he writes in *To Tirzah,* "The death of Jesus set me free." He was trying to build a New Jerusalem.

Coupling *Songs of Innocence* with *Songs of Experience,* he knew that

> by publishing the two sets of songs together, [he would] make it impossible for anyone to react sentimentally to either set. Whoever wished to babble over the natural sweetness and happiness of childhood would be reminded by *Songs of Experience* that childhood was by no means always sweet and that happiness was against Nature.[2]

Blake's *Songs* are miles away from being finger-waggingly moral, unlike those, say, of Isaac Watts, as in his *How Doth the Little Busy Bee*, the first two lines of which have stuck in folk-memory:

> How doth the little busy bee
> Improve each shining hour,
> And gather honey all the day
> From every opening flower.
>
> How skilfully she builds her cell!
> How neat she spreads her wax!
> And labours hard to store it well
> With the sweet food she makes.

In works of labour, or of skill,
I would be busy too;
For Satan finds some mischief still
For idle hands to do.

In books, or work, or healthful play,
Let my first years be past,
That I may give for every day
Some good account at last.

Like much Romantic poetry Blake's *Songs* extol joy and freedom. And here we should face certain preconceptions we may have, ones Blake is deliberately challenging. To put it simply for the moment, do we say that the *Songs of Experience* are more 'profound' than those of *Innocence* and that, in comparison, *Songs of Innocence* are 'naive', 'simplistic'? We sometimes find commentators using such words. Put it another way: is the Western mind more at home with the tragic view of life than with the comic and therefore thinks of it as being more profound? Were we to think like Blake, we would see them, like the poles of a magnet, as two counterpoised and equally valid ways of looking at the same thing.

Before encountering any of the poems, the reader must first confront the illustrated title-page with its wording "Songs of Innocence and of Experience Showing the two Contrary States of the Human Soul". This page is literally our beginning (the beginning of our experience of the book but also the beginning of human history according to the Bible). It inevitably conditions our responses to the work as a whole. The illustration is of Adam and Eve cowering, expelled from the Garden of Eden and thrown into the world of Experience, a world of hellish flame; a bird – we will see these repeatedly – representing the freedom, the innocence they have forfeited, flies above them. Both are fallen creatures and look not heavenwards but down towards the ground; Eve is in fact prostrate and Adam bends over her in a would-be protective (condoning? still loving?) manner, while at the same time holding his head for shame. We are already in the world of Experience; it's where we live. It means that any Innocence we encounter will of necessity have its being in Experience and be in consequence vulnerable and in need of protectors. Flames, as we know, can either consume or cleanse. Redemption as well as damnation is therefore implied. Though the story being told is biblical, we can, if we wish, view it as archetypal: many cultures tell a story of a lost age of perfection. It is a way of accounting for Good and Evil, a way of explaining death.

Blake's aim, as he says in *Introduction* to *Songs of Experience*, is to call on the lapsed Soul to rouse itself and "fallen, fallen light renew". "Man", he asserts, "has closed himself up till he sees all things thro' narrow chinks of his cavern." If only he could "cleanse the doors of perception everything would appear [to him] as it is, infinite".[3] This is perhaps running ahead, but it is important to establish early on the reason Blake is exploring the two contrary states of the human soul. It is to make us realise the infinite – "everything *as it is*" (my italics). This is what the piper is commanded to do – help us come to that understanding.

Next come the frontispiece and title-page of *Songs of Innocence*. The former shows the poet-shepherd (there are sheep in the picture) addressed by the visionary child. The child is free from all constraints: he floats above on a cloud; he can, as the poem tells us, vanish. And because we know "He became a little child", we naturally understand the child to be Christ – who is of course also the Good Shepherd, as well as the Pascal Lamb. We are in a world of archetypes, not of single but proliferating and even sometimes colliding meanings. Blake is not a poet of metaphor. The piper is of the earth, a protector of the sheep; they are surrounded by trees, which also protect. It is the moment of his calling, of consecration: the piper is to become a prophet and bard.

The title-page of *Songs of Innocence* shows us two children at their seated mother's knee; they are, with her guidance, reading a book, the book we ourselves are going to read. Again they are under the protection of a tree with winged guardian figures among its branches – or, seen differently, under the apple tree of Original Sin (vines circle its trunk like a serpent); the sun seems to be setting (or is a new dawn arising?). At the bottom of the page are the words "The Author & Printer W Blake".

The first poem *Introduction* (the title implies a commitment to a process) is engraved with twining vegetation to the left and right of it, with somewhat indistinct figures in each of the loops. Keynes takes this to be the Tree of Jesse, which in Isaiah purports to show the genealogy of Christ, Blake providing the piper-shepherd with a biblical ancestry. What strikes one about the poem itself is its seeming simplicity, its quatrains of fast-moving seven-syllable lines, four beats to each line, the trochaic metre giving it an air of spontaneity and enthusiastic gaiety, as do the artfully artless repetitions of "pipe"/"piper"/"piped" "sing"/"song" "and" and "so". The poem could have been written by a child or, more accurately, someone of childlike (not childish) talent. We will find the same childlike syntax and enthusiasm in *The Lamb*. Psalm 8 tells us that "Out of the mouths of babes and sucklings hast thou ordained strength". Matthew 21:16 has "Out of the mouths of babes and sucklings thou hast perfected praise" and Matthew 11:25 "Jesus answered and said, I thank thee, O Father, Lord of heaven and earth, because thou hast hid these things from the wise and prudent, and hast revealed them unto babes".

It is worth pausing here to state the obvious fact that, though Blake's poems give the impression of regularity, a syllabic count often belies this. There is great rhythmical variety on display as well as subtle artlessness.

In *Introduction* the emphasis is on happiness. The songs are of "pleasant glee"; they cause the child to laugh (laughter is infectious and can promote innocent tears of joy); the piping is one of "merry chear"; the pipe is a "happy pipe" producing "happy chear". The song is about a Lamb, in other words it is a hymn of praise. The child is actively inducting the piper into his vocation using imperatives: "pipe", "drop", "sit", "write". He has authority. They are positive as opposed to the negative commandments of the Old Testament. He tells the piper his job is to spread happiness, spread the Word, by making a song about a (capital-L) Lamb. Happiness is expansive, it redounds: we will see in other poems how it goes on and on echoing. Having given his instructions, the child vanishes as spontaneously as he appeared, leaving the piper to carry out his orders.

A process, a progression is occurring. First there is music of "pleasant glee" which becomes a wordless song about a Lamb; then the pipe is set aside and words appear. The piper is left to write these down, put them in a book so that everyone of a childlike disposition can enjoy them. Blake, in making a rural pen, is indicating clearly that he is not a writer of polite literature. The suggestion of its being unpolished is part of his democratic stance, "that *all* may read" and "*Every* child may joy to hear" (my italics).

It sounds simple. But in order to write his happy songs, a hollow reed has to be plucked and clear water has to be stained. We have been manoeuvred into thinking we are in an innocent Arcadian world. But the words "pluck'd", "hollow", "stained" provide an undercurrent of negative resonances belonging to actions associated more with Experience. I say "undercurrent" because *Introduction* is on the whole a positive and forward-looking poem. We are being asked to engage with Joy and amplify it. The poem is full of positive energy. Blake tells us in *The Marriage of Heaven and Hell* that "energy is Eternal Delight" and that "The soul of sweet delight can never be defil'd." We have begun a visionary journey through Innocence into Experience and beyond to learn the potency of these truths:

> He who binds to himself a joy,
> Does the wingèd life destroy;
> But he who kisses the joy as it flies
> Lives in eternity's sun rise.[4]

The journey is undertaken in the hope of attaining what Blake will eventually describe as "fourfold vision"[5]

## Notes

[1] Ackroyd, *Blake*.
[2] Alicia Ostriker, *Vision and Verse in William Blake* (University of Wisconsin Press, 1965).
[3] William Blake, *The Marriage of Heaven and Hell*.
[4] William Blake, *Gnomic Verses*.
[5] See chapter 13.

## 2. The lambs innocent call
### The Shepherd – The Ecchoing Green – The Lamb

The metre of *The Shepherd* is anapaestic, the rhythm jovial, "fillèd with praise". First person has been replaced by third: we, the readers, are witnesses not just to duty on the part of the shepherd but to his loving kindness. One of the *Proverbs of Hell* tells us "The most sublime act is to set another before you." We will meet this motif of selfless love again and again in *Songs*. Its supreme exemplar is of course Christ and it is the Christ-in-us Blake is at pains to call attention to and reveal.

The piper has taken on the guardianship of the flock. He is the first of the protector figures that recur throughout *Songs*. Note too that the lambs are looked after by their mothers and that, in the illustration, they are protected by a tree. After the instructions of the first poem comes the celebration of an accepted role. It is a poem of daytime – night is excluded except by implication; all is sweetness and light, tenderness and loving care, reassurance and peace. We are not in an idealised Arcadian landscape: this is the world of experience – the sheep need a devoted, watchful shepherd. This poem, like so many others, exists at a point of stasis between morn and evening, Heaven and Hell, life and death.

The illustration shows a shepherd who has replaced his pipe with a crook, the symbol of his guardianship. A bird, like the dove of the Holy Ghost, flies reassuringly over the scene.

*The Ecchoing Green*'s effect is one of spontaneous energy – of bells ringing (chiming/rhyming), birds singing, children innocently playing, everything echoing. The poem, spoken by a child, celebrates the human flock, the interconnecting community, at peace on the village green, everyone welcoming Spring. The old folk have a natural place here and take pleasure in remembering their own youth; they are as much

13

part of the scene and the natural cycle that ends with rest in the evening as are the happy children. Laughter and its echoes fill the place. Laughter redounds, it removes "care", and is an aspect of praise, but, again, night is looming and children, like birds in their nests, have to seek the protection of their mothers and bedtime.

The poem is spread over two engraved pages. In the first the green is dominated by a sturdy oak under which the old ones sit. Centrally placed is a mother lovingly caring for her two children, one of whom has buried its head in her lap, perhaps in sorrow. There are two boys playing with a bat and a hoop. These are seen in the next page's illustration climbing a vine to pluck its grapes. Are they, as Keynes suggests, already on the road to experience? The children below them (one with a bat, another with a kite) remain innocent for the time being.

It is worth noting that the twining of vines and tendrils in Blake's illustrations is not simply there for decorative effect but to denote movement and growth – in Blake's word, progression.

*The Lamb* is a real test. With its reminder of Matthew 18:1–3, it challenges our sense of ourselves, of our self-worth. Matthew 18 says:

1. At that time came the disciples unto Jesus, saying, Who is the greatest in the kingdom of heaven?
2. And Jesus called a little child unto him, and set him in the midst of them.
3. And said, Verily I say unto you, except ye be converted and become as little children, ye shall not enter into the kingdom of heaven.

The problem with *The Lamb* is that, as a well-anthologised piece, it has, like *The Tyger*, become detached from its context and sentimentally associated with hymns like 'All things bright and beautiful', 'Jesus wants me for a sunbeam'. There is nothing sentimental to it. Its truths are simple, not simplistic; the child-speaker is innocent, not naive. Nor is it a matter of age or gender. It is the child-in-us, whatever age.

The child of the poem (the child-in-us) is simply unstoppably eager, as real children often are, to communicate and share something important to him/her. Not just that: each of the two ten-line stanzas ends with a blessing that affirms and confirms the joyful sharing of Good News. In *Proverbs of Hell* Blake tells us that "Bless relaxes". In contrast to *The Tyger* where questions are asked and no answers given, here the questions are playfully rhetorical, the answers, though provided by the child and secure in his/her conviction, are already known – the lamb has no way of replying and, in any case, would have no chance of doing so, so non-stop eager is the child in his/her desire to share. The opening and closing two lines of each stanza give a feeling of roundness – arrived-at, not-to-be-gainsaid completion.

This is the voice of delight. There is a real sense of intimacy in the poem, of innocence in practice, spreading the Word. And the Word has its own logic. It is not one of reason but of association and symbolism and, of course, absolute faith. Lamb = child = Christ = child = lamb – all of them embodiments of Innocence. One might adopt a word from Catholic liturgy and call it transubstantiation. It all makes perfect sense. It is the way poets think; understanding this is important in reading Blake.

The illustration shows a child with a flock of sheep beside a cottage, on the roof of which two doves perch; another bird flies upwards. Sapling trees surround and overhang the scene.

# 3. O! my soul is white
## *The Little Black Boy – The Blossom – The Chimney Sweeper – The Little Boy Lost – The Little Boy Found*

In *The Little Black Boy* Blake gives a voice to someone from outside the sort of social community at ease in *The Ecchoing Green*. Exploitation is one of Blake's themes, one of the activities of Experience. Our black boy is one of the potentially exploited. Living in the southern wild, he is a more-than-likely candidate for the slave trade. He too is found to be living at a crossroads-moment, between freedom and slavery, life and death. The topic of slavery is one layer in the poem but we must not limit its impact to this. There are others. We will more and more see that the aim of Experience is to corrupt, exploit, and constrain Innocence. Experience is the realm of the predatory agents of a false God, his priests and his king. Like the child in the previous poem, the little black boy's voice is the voice of Innocence but whereas in *The Lamb* the child's innocence evokes feelings of warmth, security and goodness, the little black boy's is heartbreaking: he thinks his blackness bereaves him of light and that his way of being part of the human community is to engage with his mother's explanation of God's arrangement of the Universe. Her message may not be Christian but it is nonetheless the same message: we pass through mortal life, learning to bear the beams of love, finally to gather, rejoicing in an after-life, round God's golden tent. Blake is insisting on the ideal of universal brotherhood as well as revealing paradise to us. This is explicit in *The Divine Image* where he states:

And all must love the human form,
In heathen, turk or jew.
Where Mercy, Love & Pity dwell,
There God is dwelling too.

There is also therefore a political layer as well as a social and religious. 'Meanings' in Blake are multiple and all one and the same. I have put 'meanings' into inverted commas because we castrate poems when we reduce them to formulae or simple answers. The poet and critic Geoffrey Grigson has this to say:

If poems are 'about' – if they are about artichokes, or the Cape of Good Hope, or God, this aboutness amounts in each poem only to a permeating element.[1]

As with the chimney sweeper we are about to meet, the little black boy uncomplainingly accepts, with his mother's explanation of it, his condition. Her wisdom helps him bear the beams of love. But that is not the end of the story:

And thus I say to little English boy.
When I from black and he from white cloud free,
And round the tent of God like lambs we joy:

I'll shade him from the heat till he can bear,
To lean in joy upon our father's knee.
And then I'll stand and stroke his silver hair,
And be like him and he will then love me.

What seems impossible in this mortal life is 'natural' in the after-life, Eternity. This is told to us in poem after poem. We are all equal in the eyes of Eternity. The black boy, like the child in *The Lamb*, is simply expressing this truth and using the same kind of 'logic', based here upon the interrelationship between notions of black and white. There is touching irony in the fact that he thinks himself more prepared for Heaven than the little English boy. In Blake's universe black is more often associated with night, the time the predators appear. But to see this as exclusively so is to give in to dualistic thinking. In this poem black is, startlingly, an aspect of Innocence. The black boy will take upon himself the role of Christ to comfort and aid the little white boy. Again age is not a criterion: the black boy will stroke the white boy's "silver hair". Not even an agnostic can fail to be moved (and to tears) by this. And once we put the chimney sweepers into the picture we are forced to take on board a great irony: namely that some English (white) boys are, because of their trade – their form of slavery – black in appearance. As with them, the little black boy is an inexhaustible fund of love.

The poem has seven quatrains rhyming ABAB and this time in pentameters, ironically the metre the English ear is mostly at home with. It is spread over two engraved pages, the first of which shows the mother and child under a tree hailing the blazing sun. In the second, two boys stand before an attentive, haloed Christ holding his crook in his arm. Again, a protecting tree bends over them.

*The Blossom* seems on the surface a simple enough poem but there are, I think, problems. The first question to ask is: who is actually speaking: the blossom or a tree? Is the blossom part of the tree or something a tree observes? Or is it the blossom that witnesses the events of the poem? The title might well suggest the blossom is the speaker, but this is complicated by the word 'my' which, to my ears, suggests something other.

What occurs in the poem? We have two verses of six lines each. They suggest the kind of balance that, as we've already said, denotes a form of stasis, what T.S. Eliot calls "the still point of the turning world"[2]. The rhythm is irregular. In verse one the speaker addresses a sparrow who has swiftly targeted its nest, while in verse two a robin is addressed – it has also found its nest but, unlike the merry sparrow, is heard sobbing. Is this a parallel to the two children we see on the first page of *The Ecchoing Gtreen*, one of them with its head buried in its mother's lap? Does the sparrow represent Innocence and the robin the damaged (fallen) state of Experience? Has the sparrow, as in the nursery rhyme, killed cock robin? Is the red breast of the robin meant to remind us of traditional associations with Christ's blood spilled from the Cross onto the bird's breast? Is it sobbing because it too has suffered a mortal wound? All this would be fine if it weren't for the fact that the condition of both birds makes the blossom "happy". Is it happy in welcoming and admiring the sparrow's energy and innocence; and is it equally happy in being able to provide comfort to the sobbing robin? Have we here the two contrary states of the human soul? If the speaker is a tree, is it the Tree of Life – Christ welcoming both innocent and the hurt to his bosom? This seems to me to be the most feasible. I am not in sympathy with Keynes' Freudian commentary on the illustration, which interprets its swirling tree-shaped flames as "an organ of generation" ejaculating tiny winged figures into the bosom of a maiden in a green dress perched on one of the branches. Is the poem *really* about the "consummation of love by the act of generation"?

Like *The Little Black Boy*, *The Chimney Sweeper* is a heart-rending poem. Its rhythms are colloquial Cockney ("There's little Tom Dacre, who cried when his head/That curl'd like a lambs back, was shav'd, so I said ..."). It is hard to say this aloud without wanting to put on an accent of some kind. You certainly cannot say it without tenderness in your voice.

The heartbreaking aspect of the poem is that, just like the black boy, the chimney sweeper gives an account of his condition as 'normal', with no hint of accusation whatsoever. Where we would expect recrimination, even outrage, we find acceptance ... which actually hurts more. Both boys and the speaker's fellow sufferers are cheered by the consolations of Heaven and a life in Eternity. And of course the Christian message *is* just this. The key to the poem lies in the friction between what the speaker tells the reader and how the reader would conventionally respond. We must learn to be sensitive to Blake's occasional use of irony. The reader is caught in an hypocrisy: "So *your* chimneys I sweep & in soot I sleep" (my italics). We are inescapably complicit. (Note that the chimney sweeper has no mother and that his father sold him into this form of slavery. Fathers come off badly in *Songs*; mothers, until we get to *To Tirzah*, are usually treated positively). How, without appreciating its irony, can we read the poem's final line?

So if all do their duty, they need not fear harm.

This is the voice of society, of "you, hypocrite lecteur"[3] It is also, ironically, the voice of the speaker of the poem, who is likely to be a little older than Tom and had time to accept his condition, while at the same time, like a substitute father, looking out for poor Tom. He has been brainwashed into accepting society's shibboleths: don't cause trouble and you won't receive any trouble. But of course there is further irony: the statement is actually true in the context of Eternity. Tom Dacre has had the reassurance of his dream (vision) of freedom, play, laughter, with sins washed away; he *will* "have God for his father & never want joy". The coffins of black are both the chimneys and imprisonment in earthly mortality. Ackroyd sums it up as "the plight of all mankind trapped in their mortal bodies and longing to be free". "The blackened and sooty body of the young child", he says, "becomes an emblem of the body itself, the coffin carried with us everywhere."[4] The dream, like the little black boy's mother's words, is a real consolation. The chimney sweepers can live with the real promise of reward in Heaven. This is not a kind of fatalism: accept the status quo, conform and you'll be OK. It doesn't let society off the hook. "Except ye ... become as little children, ye shall not enter the kingdom of heaven." But it does open the world up to hope.

Fear of being lost is a very real fear among children. I can remember, as a small child, being taken into a big department store in Liverpool, and experiencing real terror at suddenly not seeing where I thought my mother would be. Bad dreams have a similar effect.

20

*The Little Boy Lost* shows us another child abandoned by his father. In the first quatrain he gives voice to his anguish. This is not a poem of acceptance. The father is no loving-tender shepherd and the child's anguished words are lost in the wind. It is a bad dream of abandonment – in the second quatrain he is exposed to dreadful darkness, to the wild elements, to being bogged down in mud, to the manic swirling of vapours. (I don't think the last line means that the vapours disappeared – the mists lifting – but that they swirled menacingly like wicked sprites.) This is very much like a child having a nightmare in which its worst fears (of being lost and powerless) are realised. It is also at a deeper level a success story for Satan.

It is at this point we might find it useful to understand that Blake thought in terms of two divinities: the God of the Old Testament and the God of the New. The former is the God of Prohibitions (of Thou-Shalt-Not) and of Vengeance, the embodiment of Cruelty, Jealousy ("For I, the Lord, your God, am a jealous God")[5], Terror and Secrecy; the latter New Testament God is Christ whose Sermon-on-the-Mount pronouncements are positive and affirmative (for example "Thou shalt love thy neighbour as thyself").[6] Christ embodies the qualities of Mercy, Pity, Peace and Love. The former is the God of false religion and the Devil in disguise: he is the Ancient of Days in Blake's famous painting, white-haired and white-bearded holding a pair of compasses which also look like lightning. Blake will call him Urizen (Your Reason or to some commentators Horizon) because he embodies the mechanical philosophies of Locke and Newton;[7] he also calls him Nobodaddy (nobody's father). "Why art thou silent and invisible/Father of jealousy?/Why dost thou hide thyself in clouds/From every searching Eye?"[8]

So the father in this poem is not just a particular child's parent, he is also Satan whose job is to confound us.

The rhythm, in contrast to the boy's plodding through mire, is fast-moving, staccato.

*The Little Boy Found* feels as if it runs on regular lines. In it the child wakes up to comfort and reassurance. Is the "wand'ring light" leading him astray (a Will o' the Wisp?) or leading him home to where his mother has been in anguish over him? Now God, dressed in the whiteness of purity, appears and saves him (save as in salvation) and brings him safely to his mother. The boy's parental father turns into his real Father – the Good Shepherd who is always nigh. The child has had his visionary glimpse of the fallen world of experience with its sorrow, weeping, its lonelinesses, but also its promise of rescue.

In the illustration to the first poem we see the child following a strange blazing light deeper into the forest. In the second the child is being led out of the darkness by a haloed Christ (made to look androgynous – beyond gender); the child too has a halo (he is one of the saved). Below, to the right of the poem, is the figure of his mother raising her arms in welcome – something we may wish to remember when we look at the illustration to *Infant Sorrow*.

**Notes**
1 Geoffrey Grigson, *The Private Art* (Allison & Busby, 1982).
2 T.S. Eliot, *Four Quartets* (Faber, 1944).
3 Baudelaire as quoted by T.S. Eliot in his poem *The Waste Land* (Hogarth Press, 1922).
4 Ackroyd, *Blake*.
5 Exodus 20:4–5.
6 Matthew 19:19
7 When he reread his Newton and Locke, Blake wrote in *Marginalia* (notes in the margins of books): "I felt the same Contempt & Abhorrence then that I do now. They mock Inspiration & Vision. Inspiration & Vision was then & and now is & I hope will always remain my Element, my Eternal Dwelling place." Blake also painted Newton wielding compasses.
8 William Blake, *To Nobodaddy*.

# 4. Come live & be merry

*Laughing Song – A Cradle Song –*
*The Divine Image*

After nightmare and waking from it, it is time to rejoice.
*Laughing Song* does that. It is also, however, again a test in
which our own particular degree of innocence is challenged and
measured. We are invited to join in. But do we have the "sweet
round mouths" that can, without embarrassment, sing "Ha, Ha,
He"? How much of Cruelty, Jealousy, Terror and Secrecy,
inhibiting us, is implanted in our hearts? Can we feel
comfortable in the scene? We can always retreat from it claiming
it as a kind of nostalgia.[1]

In this poem Blake offers us an animated landscape in
which everything is dynamically in a state of laughter: woods,
stream, air, hills, meadows, grasshopper, birds and three little
girls called Mary, Susan and Emily. It is picnic time, a social
occasion: there are cherries and nuts to eat. Laughter is
nature singing spontaneously, innocently – is a hymn of praise
to its Maker. It is infectious; everyone is at it, and we are asked
to join in. Can we add our laughter to the scene? The
instruction is simple enough: come live and be merry, but is
this something costing, in the words of T.S. Eliot, "not less
than everything"?[2]

The poem has again a jovial rhythmical pulse. The
illustration shows eight young people gathered round a table
under the shade of a tree. One of them is standing with his back
to us raising the cheer, a hat in one hand, a glass in the other.

Compared to the open-air joviality of *Laughing Song*,
*A Cradle Song* gives us the quiet, intimate and hypnotic
tenderness of a lullaby: a mother singing to her sleeping child,
asking for blessings to be poured on its head and for it to be
protected from the sort of nightmare the little boy lost

experienced. The words "sweet" and "sleep" are repeated over and over like a charm. The night in which predators appear requires safeguards to be put in place: the mother herself smiling over the child, the moon, an Angel mild – all there to "beguile", a word Blake uses several times in *Songs* not in its sense of fraudulently cheating but in its meaning of "to charm; to wile on, or into any course ... to divert attention in some pleasant way from" (*The Shorter Oxford English Dictionary*). Nocturnal predators are by no means eliminated but they can be put off the scent. So there is an undercurrent of precariousness in the poem. The mother tells the child that "all creation slept", referring to the seventh day of Creation and therefore, by extension, to the imminent Fall. Is this the reason for the mother's weeping? She has prescience, knows that sacrifice is involved? Christ, as the poem clearly states, wept for man's sinfulness. The first illustration shows tangled vegetation; the second a curtained room with a woman leaning over a cradle in which a haloed child is sleeping. Is this the same child we meet in *Infant Sorrow*? In one sense, yes.

Blake makes explicit his perception of the divine in the human, "looking through instead of with the eyes".[3] The mother sees Christ's image in the face of her child and, just like the child in *The Lamb*, sets out the equation Lamb = Child = Christ. The poem prepares us for what comes next – namely *The Divine Image*, which states unequivocally that the true God is compounded of four great virtues, Mercy, Pity, Peace and Love. (We do well to note the use of the definite article in the title so as to compare it with *A Divine Image* later). The four virtues manifest themselves in human form in Christ made man. As Hazard Adams rightly says, "Man is ... a microcosm of God and, therefore, God himself or a reflection of God in particular terms." It was Blake's conviction that "behind the characteristics of each man there exist the lineaments of the 'eternal man'",[4] the human form divine which all men inhabit and all religions should acknowledge:

And every man of every clime,
That prays in his distress,
Prays to the human form divine
Love Mercy Pity Peace.[5]

The illustration shows swirling flames similar to those of *The Blossom*. The pair we saw on the title page is being raised up from the earth by Christ; at the top of the picture they are received by an angel in green.

## Notes

[1] I am grateful to John Lucas for reminding me of the fashion in 18th century painting for dressing children and women up as shepherdesses, as was sometimes done by painters like Gainsborough and Reynolds for whom Blake had only contempt.

[2] Eliot, *Four Quartets*.

[3] Hazard Adams, *Reading Blake's Lyrics: 'The Tyger'*, first published in Texas Studies in Literature and Language II (University of Texas Press, 1960).

[4] John Beer, *Blake's Humanism*, (Manchester University Press, 1968).

[5] Note the approximate rhymes here (and elsewhere) – acceptable in songs.

# 5. Then come home my children
## *Holy Thursday – Night – Spring – Nurse's Song*

Outside the smiling nursery, out in the streets of the big city, poorhouse children are being treated differently, "treated" to a special "holy" day in which they are allowed to offer thanksgiving for being looked after by the state. They are permitted – strictly regimented – to enter St Paul's Cathedral, built by Wren a century earlier to look more like a palace or a pagan temple than a church. The poem consists of three quatrains of mainly fourteeners, with a caesura normally after the eighth syllable. It has a march-like rhythm which parodies the regulated procession of the children into the cathedral. It also suggests an army on the move, literally a salvation army. The illustration depicts the boys and girls, strictly segregated, walking in twos, like the animals going into the Ark – also to be 'saved'.

And yet they possess a spontaneity, they have their radiance – or is this the complacent perception of the onlooking narrator? Do they raise their hands and sing so lustily because they have been drilled? The grey-headed beadles and the aged, philanthropic men – as wise guardians of the poor – are there not to surround them with loving-kindness, like shepherds with their flocks, but to keep them in a condition of conformity, obedient to both state and the false God whose classical temple they are in. "Innocence dwells with Wisdom but never with Ignorance" Blake says in one of his *Proverbs of Hell*. If this is so, then *Holy Thursday* is a deeply ironic poem in which complacent conventional response to the sight is caught out saying, without its knowing it, the real truth contained in "Then cherish pity; lest you drive an angel from your door", a truth emphasised in Hebrews 13:2 in the words "Be not forgetful to entertain strangers, for thereby some have entertained angels unawares." The service is an annual one (one day out of 365); for the rest of the time the children go back to the kind of conditions we are so familiar with from Dickens. You can always engage one to sweep your chimneys, imagining you are committing yourself to an act of charity. But as Blake tells us in *The Human Abstract*, "Pity would be no more,/If we did not make somebody poor."

The indications of order, pattern, number, regulation are there in the architecture, things Blake despised. And yet set against this is the children's innocent radiance, their spontaneous singing – we cannot escape this. They "flow" like the Thames, they have the energy of a mighty wind, their voices reach Heaven. The lines are full of biblical resonances which leave no doubt that these lambs with innocent hands, represent the power of latent revolution. As John Lucas has written, "... not to see how *Holy Thursday* pulses with the joy of such energy, is to deny its politics and thus to denature the poem."[1]

Night is when it is normal to rest and sleep and for sleepers to be watched over. In the poem *Night* we are in similar territory to that of *A Cradle Song* but the canvas is broader. The speaker is aware of the need for various protective figures – the moon, guardian angels – and rejoices in and is comforted by their presence. They cannot always prevent predators appearing and wanting to feed. But death, for Blake, was no more than a door into Eternity. And so when the wolves and tigers kill their prey the angels simply receive souls and transport them to Heaven, as the chimney sweepers are in Tom Dacre's dream. It is in this way all contraries are reconciled since, in Heaven, as the Bible explicitly states: "The wolf also shall dwell with the lamb, and the leopard shall lie down with the kid; and the calf and the young lion and the fatling together; and a little child shall lead them" (Isaiah 11:6).

By the end of the poem, the speaker has turned into a grazing golden lion. Blake says in *The Marriage of Heaven and Hell* (what greater reconciling of contraries can you get!):

1. Man has no Body distinct from his Soul; for that call'd Body is a portion of Soul discern'd by the five Senses, the chief inlets of Soul in this age.
2. Energy is the only life, and is from the Body; and Reason is the bound or outward Circumference of Energy.
3. Energy is Eternal delight.

The poet knew two worlds, those of earth and eternity, time and vision, human and divine, knowing that they were really all one. Imagination for him was no surrender to mere fanciful thought but a sacred place of visionary significance.

There are two pages to *Night.* The illustration to the first shows a lion with winged figures above him, with others among the branches of a tree; in the second we see five angels receiving the spirits of the dead with three more among branches, through which stars are seen shining.

Taken out of context, *Spring* might be considered a primitive poem: crudely written, rhythmically inept, driven by tumbling rhymes – just as my own first poems, made up simply of rhymes, at the age of nine were. On the other hand, you might (and I'm confident Blake wants us to) say it is driven by sheer delight – which he knows we find difficult. We want complexity. As with *Laughing Song,* the reader is being assessed. Are we ready (i.e. innocent enough) to welcome the springtime of a new life? A possible question remains: are we meant to pick up a reference to Peter's betrayal of Christ in the line "Cock does crow"? If so, it has to be subliminal for the reason that the poem as a whole is an expression of the energy of eternal delight mentioned above. How do we resist the temptation to dismiss it as 'naive'? Why is a song of joy seen to be less profound than one of sorrow? *Spring* reinforces the 'message' of previous poems: that it's good to be alive once you realise life is eternal. The poem also takes up two pages. In the illustration to the first we see a mother with a child on her knee reaching out toward lambs, with small winged figures below them among the spirals that enfold the words of the poem; the second shows a child alone among sheep fondling a lamb, with, above them, again winged figures.

In *Nurse's Song* we find one of the ubiquitous protectors of children overanxious about the oncoming night and asking her charges to cease their play. She lives in the consciousness of Time, whereas they inhabit Eternity, the two worlds Blake constantly dovetails, creating a dialectic between them, making us see them as, in the words of Keith Sagar, "co-related states ... complementary but conflicting".[2] The children 'know better': there is still time for play; their instincts are right, so the nurse lets them play "till the light fades away"'. In the illustration we find the nurse watching the children as they dance in a circle; there is a weeping willow to the right with its suggestion that sorrow is never far away.

As in *The Ecchoing Green*, the universe is in a state of reverberating, amplified laughter, a place of spontaneity and freedom. The poem's rhythms bound along joyfully, especially the jubilant last two lines:

> The little ones leapèd & shouted & laughed
> And all the hills ecchoèd.

**Notes**

[1] John Lucas, *England and Englishness* (Hogarth Press, 1990).
[2] Keith Sagar, http://www.keithsagar.co.uk/Blake/index.html. Sagar extends this to "two dialectically arranged aspects not just of the human psyche, but within and behind all Creation itself".

## 6. Sweet joy befall thee
### *Infant Joy – A Dream – On Anothers Sorrow*

Of *Infant Joy's* fifty words, 46 are monosyllables; the poem is characteristically constructed of repeated words and phrases. The reader is witness to an exuberance[1] of "happy", "Joy", "sweet", "pretty". It is as if the child from *A Cradle Song* is awake and given a voice, its own precious individuality. In a sense it is a baptismal poem but one in which the child determines its own name. Again, as in *The Lamb* and *The Little Black Boy,* we find Innocence obeying its own 'logic': Joy = happiness = child = child's name. We might also include the consonance of rhyme in the equation. This is quite different from thinking dualistically: Blake requires an alternative mode of thinking, one opposed to Baconian/Newtonian/Lockean reason. As Peter Marshall has pointed out, "Blake was convinced that their mechanical philosophy made the cardinal error of separating the perceiving mind from the object of perception, the observer from the observed."[2] Here child, mother, guardian angel (see illustration) and reader are all fixed in a moment that is both in time and beyond time, in the Now of Eternity. The obvious thing to note is that child and the adult-other speak on equal terms. This is one of those poems which, if you weren't aware of the illustration, you might think is a conversation between parent and child. The illustration however shows the child addressing an angel. It is not, as Keynes, suggests, an "annunciation": the child is already born. We see the threesome enclosed in the swirling flame-red petals of a flower, clearly denoting energy and aspiration, as well as possibly suggesting the security of the womb.

As we have noted in other poems, there is, however, a subtext of anxiety. The child has been born into the world of Experience, the dimensions of time ("two days old") and place.

It needs its protectors. The blessing "Sweet joy befall thee!" is subjunctive in mood, a wish rather than prophecy, and the line "I sing the while" introduces the notion of duration, suggesting 'as long as I am able or it is necessary'. The child will become subject to the repressions of the Moral Law and will encounter not just the selfless love of Innocence but also the selfish love of Experience. *Songs of Innocence* may offer a child's-eye view of the world but there is nothing simplistic about it. If the poems speak of transcendence, the vision is tempered by knowledge of the ways of the world. What we have found is that Innocence is, in its mortal form, vulnerable.

In the next poem *A Dream*, the speaker (the child of *A Cradle Song* whose bed is also angel-guarded?) recounts a dream in which an ant loses its way in the dark. This is a child's dream in which events are miniaturised (ant/glow-worm/beetle) in a cartoon-like fashion. It is a dream we have already encountered in which fear of being separated from a parent ("O my children! Do they cry?") is re-enacted. We should note the characteristics of Experience here: struggle, darkness, tangled sprays, sorrow. Tearful pity is evoked. But calamity is averted, we have a happy ending. There are protecting spirits, humbly personified agents of divine compassion, able to guide the ant back to her home, her sighing husband, and her weeping children.

*On Anothers Sorrow* is strategically placed, a summation, a spelling out and making definite of all we have so far encountered. These are the lessons we have been shown, truths we are required to learn, and this is how we should put them into practice. Sorrow, like laughter, is infectious: it is impossible not to share in it. It is not really a matter of choice: the emphatically repeated 'never' declares it to be imperative. We should follow the example of Christ who, in becoming a child, brought joy into the world, and who, as a man of woe, understands what sorrow is. He is ever-present, watching over us while we learn to bear the beams of love. Joy can destroy grief. Blake uses his favourite quatrain form of seven syllables per line with couplet rhyming. But the tone this time is one of painfully honest self-exposure: its rhetorical questions have answers spelt out, clearly delineated, and its emphatic instructions, its repetitions are unequivocal and deny gainsaying. The poem, like all the others in *Innocence*, is addressed to the child-in-us. The piper has, as directed, provided something – even if it is hard for us to accommodate – which every child may joy to hear.

**Notes**

[1] In *Proverbs of Hell* Blake tells us that "Exuberance is Beauty."
[2] Peter Marshall, *William Blake, Visionary Anarchist,* (Freedom Press, 1988).

# 7. O Earth return! *Songs of Experience*
## *Introduction – Earth's Answer*

The frontispiece to *Songs of Experience* is a puzzle. It shows the piper of *Songs of Innocence* purposefully striding forward, with a haloed and winged child balanced on his head. Is he about to "leave leave his flock behind and advance into a state of experience" (Keynes)? Is this the same child that appeared on the cloud or the cherub Keynes thinks might come from Ezekiel 28:14, therefore representing "the corruption following Experience"? Does the ivy encircling the tree on the right indicate troubles ahead? There is certainly determination on the face of the piper. Is it the determination to fulfil his role as prophet/bard and rouse the Earth from its sleep of death?

The lettering on the title-page of *Songs of Innocence* is free-flowing; that of *Songs of Experience* is in hard-edged, forbidding capitals. The illustration shows two young people bending over and mourning the death of parents, in a monumental tomb designed with hard, heavy, straight lines.

The figures inhabiting the illustrations to *Songs of Experience* tend to cling to the earth in attitudes of sorrow – huddling, kneeling, stooping or sometimes prostrate; those of *Innocence* are normally upright or seated or in movement (play, dance) – with them there's a sense of sharing, of being part of a community. One of Blake's *Proverbs of Hell* tells us, "The bird a nest, the spider a web, man friendship." Again I am grateful to John Lucas for the acute observation that the poems in *Innocence* have a tendency to deploy the present tense and those of *Experience* the past tense.

We have seen the plight of mankind already adumbrated in *Songs of Innocence*. The world of Innocence is, as Ackroyd says, a "spiritual world interfused with energy and power"[1] but it is always precariously poised on the edge of being corrupted, exploited by the satanic forces of Cruelty, Jealousy, Terror and Secrecy. It is into this world Blake now plunges us. We are already armed to meet it – that is if we see *Songs of Innocence* as pre-emptive. Perhaps the piper's striding forward is meant to encourage us into joining him in his mission to build a New Jerusalem.

It's no easy job. The scale is cosmic. The illustration to *Introduction* has the poem floating on a cloud (obfuscating "clouds of reason") surrounded by the stars of the universe. At the bottom of the page, Earth, a female figure, reclines on a couch.

In *Introduction* the declamatory voice of the bard/prophet,[2] whose vision transcends the bounds of time and who has heard God talking to Adam ("the lapsèd Soul") both before and after the Fall (Adam once perfect, now wretchedly fallen, as all who read their Bibles – i.e. the "Holy Word" – also know), urges a reluctant Earth ("Why wilt thou turn away") to embrace a new dawn, the beginning of a new age, and arise like the morn from "the slumberous mass" of physicality and corruption into the spiritual vision of Eternity. Earth is advised that time is running out and told her resentment is perverse. In this poem, sleep is not a part of the natural cycle but a form of wilful denial. The lapsed Soul can, if it would only realise, bring about its own salvation. To do so it needs to reject its subjugation to false ideas (Reason) and false religion (the Church of Urizen).

*Earth's Answer* reveals Earth in thrall to Satan. The illustration shows the poem encircled by a snake. Earth can still hear the "Father of the ancient men" – the true God – but confuses him with the "selfish father of men", the God of the Old Testament, the Devil in disguise. She understands her plight (consciousness is part of her agony) and wishes for her chains to be broken, but seems more intent on blame than action, on self-pitying, angry protestation. Selfish love and sexual repression are part of her complaint. Worst of all, she

34

blindly thinks her plight ("bane") is Eternal. The poem is staccato in its rhythms and made up of disjointed fragments that suggest she is no longer coherent, that the Universe is resorting to its primal chaos. Both poems follow similar formal patterns: Earth attempting to answer the Bard in kind but proving herself less articulate.

*Introduction* to *Innocence* needed no opposing voice: the piper obeyed the child on the cloud and became the shepherd watching over his flock. The first two poems of *Experience* suggest a kind of schizophrenia.

**Notes**
1 Ackroyd, *Blake.*
2 Cf the opening stanzas of *The Little Girl Lost.*

# 8. A Hell in Heavens despite

## *The Clod and the Pebble – Holy Thursday –*
## *The Little Girl Lost – The Little Girl Found –*
## *The Chimney Sweeper*

What do we say of a poem like *The Clod and the Pebble* beyond marvelling at its wonderful (fearful) symmetry in which two opposite views of love are held in perfect balance, in stasis, in virtual deadlock? It is Blake's way of fixing us at a moment of choice, like travellers brought to a signpost offering two directions. The poem unequivocally means what it says and directly says itself.

The choice is simple: either Heaven or Hell, in which – either way – as warring states of soul, we actively participate.[1] Equally balanced powers competing with one another. On the one hand there is selfless love, which we have had occasion to meet over and over in *Songs of Innocence* as our most potent weapon against Satan; on the other, there is selfish love with its sadistic subjugation of others, the enemy of all that is good. Selfless love is the burden of the humble Clod of Clay's song, whereas the smooth, polished Pebble's is heard as something "warbled" in "metres meet". We know from Blake's espousal of the popular tradition of ballads, hymns, nursery rhymes that he is, in the kind of writing he undertakes (and politically), on the side of the Clod of Clay. "Warbled" and "metres meet" suggest the sophistications of polite literature of a different class altogether. The Clod doesn't warble, it simply sings.

The illustration shows, above the poem, cattle (Experience?) and sheep (Innocence?) drinking from a stream, which is either the river of life or, if you agree with Keynes, the water of materialism. Below the poem are a duck, a frog and a worm, "each in turn preying on the other".

There is a tendency for some of the poems of *Experience* to adopt a rhetorical tone. *Holy Thursday* in *Innocence* self-indulgently applauded, in an easy-going colloquial tone, the sight and sound of the "flowers of London town" trooping into St Paul's. This is society congratulating itself. In the *Holy Thursday* of *Experience* Blake goes public, demanding attention, as a preacher might denouncing evil.

He starts with four rhetorical questions, to which emphatic answers are given. England may be a "rich and fruitful land" materially, but spiritually it is impoverished. Smugness is replaced by outrage; the children trooping into St Paul's are declared victims of a "usurous"' society which imprisons them in the "eternal winter" of Experience. But Blake also knows there is an alternative. And the choice is ours, either to build a Hell in Heaven's despite or a Heaven in Hell's despair. If the world were attuned to seeing things through the eyes rather than with them, we would possess a world where spiritual hunger (and physical hunger) would have no place. The repetition of "and" (five times – reinforced by rhyming with "hand" and "land"), which appears childlike in *Innocence*, now becomes bardic outspokenness. The upper part of the illustration doesn't show the orphan children processing to St Paul's Cathedral but a mother under a bare tree gazing at the dead body of her child; further down on the right the mother is accompanied by two grieving children, below whom we see the dead child again.

Blake sees death, as we have noted, as a doorway into the next room of Eternity. And in the next two poems, *The Little Girl Lost* and *The Little Girl Found,* he is at pains to remind us of this. At the beginning the bardic/prophetic voice speaks out reassuringly ("Grave the sentence deep") of matters the first two poems have addressed – that Earth is in a state of slumber but will one day see the light and shake off sleep. The Bard now goes on to tell the story/ parable of Lyca, who at the age of seven has clearly undergone a chronic illness and died. During her illness, in which she begs for "sweet sleep" to come to her, she frets about the sorrow being caused to her parents. In death she is taken care of by visionary beasts – which, if they were in the mortal world, would treat her as their prey but which, in Heaven, if we remember the prophet Ezekiel, take her to their bosoms. In *The Little Girl Found* the parents, left behind in the world of Experience, struggle with their grief but are granted a vision, which restores their faith, of their daughter among caring beasts: Lyca will awake in Eternity and, eventually, so will they. The two poems confirm the golden joys of paradise where all contraries dissolve.

Both are constructed of thirteen (a number of bad omen) quatrains of rhyming couplets. In the first of three illustrations we see a pair of young lovers pointing to the promise contained in the first two stanzas (of plate 35 in the edition used here); above them flies a bird representing the freedom of the soul. To the right of the picture a serpent coils round a tendril of what appears to be a vine. The second illustration shows Lyca reclining under a tree, waiting to be awakened; beneath her and to the right stands a tiger, either, as Keynes would have it, scenting his victim or perhaps standing ready to welcome Lyca to "the hallow'd ground". The third illustration shows children in paradise playing with lions and tigers while Earth sleeps obliviously beside them.

*The Chimney Sweeper* in *Innocence* was heart-wrenchingly devoid of recrimination; the one of *Experience* is not. The poem denounces hypocrisy soundly by giving a victim of a corrupting, exploiting society a voice in which to speak out about his condition. Ironically the poem may be the only place he is heard. The parents who have sold him into slavery have gone to church to pray prayers of selfish love. They are the servants of the false God (Urizen = God-of-the-Old-Testament = Satan), himself served by "his Priest & King". Blake here is dangerously revealing his republican sympathies. The "heaven" (the lower case is significant) that they make of chimney sweepers' misery is not the Heaven of *The Clod and the Pebble*; it is the product of a blind personal complacency ("They think they have done me no injury").

Like the little black boy the chimney sweeper is an outsider: there is no place for him in the society that enslaves him. And yet, for all his notes of woe he is able to retain some sense of his innocence: he is, surprisingly, still able to be "happy & dance & sing". Like the children of the first *Holy Thursday* he can, despite the cold snow, hold on to what innocence he has. He is a warning to society that dissident voices such as his may contain the seeds of revolution. He is also another of our contacts with Eternity. In the illustration we see him (like Bunyan's pilgrim) with his bag on his back, walking through the snow and looking up at the clouds above him which seem to aim their dagger-like contents directly at him.

**Notes**
[1] Luke 17:20–1. "And when he was demanded of the Pharisees, when the kingdom of God should come, he answered, The kingdom of God cometh not with observation. Neither shall they say, Lo here! Or, lo there! for the kingdom of God is within you." Also of relevance is Mark 10:15 in which Christ says "Verily I say unto you, Whosoever shall not receive the kingdom of God as a little child, he shall not enter therein."

# 9. The dews of night arise
## *Nurses Song – The Sick Rose – The Fly – The Angel*

Where the nurse of *Innocence*, though naturally cautious, happily accedes to the children's joyous and truer appreciation of the division between night and day, the nurse of *Experience* is jealous, authoritarian, and cynical. The echoing laughter of play is now perceived as secretive 'whisperings'; her memories of her youth, in contrast to those of the aged in *The Ecchoing Green*, turn her face green and pale ("green" suggesting both biliousness and jealousy). Some undeclared experience in her past has distorted her vision: she turns Blake's view of innocence on its head. While concerned for the safety of her charges, she nonetheless harbours the conviction that the children are victims of deception. She ironises Blake's contention that "If the doors of perception were cleansed everything would appear to man as it is, infinite." If only the children could see what the world is 'really like' they'd know that their spring and day "are wasted in play" and simply "winter and night in disguise". In other words, they are not, as we may imagine, building a Heaven in Hell's despair. In fact the nurse is one of those building Hell. Hers is a world of fear, secrecy, cruelty – her attitudes are cruel – and jealousy. Whether she knows it or not, she serves the Jealous God of the Old Testament. The nurse of *Innocence* cares not for herself but for her children; the nurse of *Experience* is imprisoned in her own disturbed paranoid psyche. As a *Proverb of Hell* warns us, "Expect poison from the standing water."[1]

We see her in the illustration attempting to comb the hair of a young boy, perhaps to bring him reluctantly into conformity. Both appear before a doorway wreathed with vines. A young girl to the boy's right is slumped wearily on the doorstep. We can almost hear the nurse ordering the boy to stand still.

*The Sick Rose* is a jewel of a poem, a perfect miniature. E.P. Thompson rightly says that with Blake's poems we "must be prepared for seventeen types of ambiguity".[2] I mention this because, though it is far from fruitless to seek to know what the rose represents, what the nature of the sickness is, what the worm stands for, and what the relationship between rose and worm and between worm and the howling night is, we have to acknowledge that we cannot confine the poem to one set of meanings and that Blake's symbols can absorb all the meanings we can ascribe to them and more. Blake tells us in the *Proverbs of Hell* that "One thought fills immensity" and most of us know the lines from his *Auguries of Innocence* which ask us

> To see a World in a grain of sand,
> And a Heaven in a wild flower,
> Hold Infinity in the palm of your hand,
> And Eternity in an hour.

The rose can be anything – from England to the monarchy, to a person infected with venereal disease or any kind of disease, to anything considered beautiful and subject to mortality, including a real-life rose. The possibilities are endless. The worm too can accommodate a multiplicity of meanings – one of which may even be a warning that revolution is on the way.[3]

We experience poems through their formal and rhythmical energies as well as through our apprehension of 'meanings'. Though it is possible to read the opening line as having two beats (on "rose" and "sick"), I prefer to hear five heavy stresses, one for each monosyllable, as if an incontrovertible truth is being pronounced. We are in bardic mode. Line 2 has three words and two stresses: "The in*vis*ible *wórm*". The line speeds up because of the trisyllablic word "invisible" – the worm has started on its secret, deadly-earnest mission. We are not able to see the worm (which makes it even more dangerous) but we can hear the swish of its wings as it speeds on through the next two lines on its unstoppably onward movement ("swift as arrow") guaranteed by the regular pulse of stresses in "in*vi*sible", "*flies*", "*howli*ng". Then comes that extraordinary space between the two quatrains which tell us the worm has landed on target, its moment of alighting preceded by a breathless silence. Line 5 again gives us, I maintain, the five heavy uncontradictable stresses of line 1: "*Hás foúnd oút thý béd*", followed by a stunning enjambement "of crimson joy" which tells us that penetration has been effected. In the last two lines the poison begins its process of infiltration into the substance of the rose.

The word "love", after the adjectives "dark" and "secret" comes as a shock. We might expect the word 'hatred' to be more appropriate. It is a love poem! The relationship of worm to rose is one of love, and the love is seen to be destructive. A question we may ask is" are the rose and the worm necessary to each other's existence? In another word, is it a matter of symbiosis? The way the stress falls on the final word of the poem is masterly. The deed is done, there is no way back. We are at the moment of death. The rose's mortality is assured. As Hamlet's mother tells him, "all that lives must die,/Passing through nature to eternity."

*The Sick Rose* is a perfect example of a poem which, with the positioning of its words, its stresses, its rhythmical energies, its formal discipline, dynamically enacts what it is 'about'. A poem as an event and not the record of an event. The illustration shows a rose cankered and brought to the ground, strange-looking creatures crawling along thorny stems bending earthwards. A human figure tries vainly to escape from the rotting flower.

*The Fly* is a problematic poem. At first reading you would think it properly belonged in *Songs of Innocence*. Its "summer's play" aligns it with Innocence; the fly, too, presumably in its way, dances, drinks and sings.

Further readings, however, expose ambiguities.[4] Positioned immediately after *The Sick Rose*, it would appear to serve the function of reminding us that death is nothing to be unhappy about, a step into another room. Does the "thoughtless hand", like the invisible worm, destroy or, to put it more positively, bring an end to mortality? All creatures have their share of life; all pass through nature to eternity. Does this enable Blake to express the equation "Am not I/A fly like thee?/Or art not thou/A man like me?" Does "brush'd away" signify that the narrator has killed the fly or merely sent it packing? Does "thoughtless" mean the act is a spontaneous one? (In *The Marriage of Heaven and Hell* we find the statement that "Jesus was all virtue, and acted from impulse, not from rules"). Or does it suggest regret and culpability? If thought can be equated with consciousness, do the speaker and the fly both possess it? Or does the speaker envy the fly for its lack of this faculty? Is the fly as much a candidate for Heaven? The poem is not a lament for the transience or loss of life – even if the fly's life is more transient than a man's. Time is collapsed in the poem; the speaker clearly sees everything "as it is, infinite". Life and death are held again in balance. The readiness is all.

Flies are conventionally regarded as disease-carrying pests and associated with the Devil. Does the poem challenge these preconceptions? Blake talks to the fly in a kindly way, seemingly on equal terms. The illustration comes as a surprise: like *Nurses Song*, it shows a woman and two children, both this time female. One of them is playing shuttlecock (is this innocent play or is she swatting a fly?). We cannot be sure whether the adult female, holding both arms of a younger child to form a circle, is playing or restraining.

*The Angel* reports a dream, which is to be taken as a prophetic warning. It is a variation on the *carpe diem* theme of "gather ye rosebuds while ye may." It is, on one level, about sexual repression or sexual rejection, pre-echoed in *Earth's Answer* in the mention of the "virgins of youth and morning"; it foreshadows the Youth and the Virgin of *Ah! Sunflower*. It could be the nurse of *Experience* talking. Having, in the dream, hidden her "heart's delight" from her Angel – who as a result leaves her – she imprisons herself in her own self-justifications, arms herself defensively against love, with the consequence the she is to die an old maid. This is the prospect the dream projects. A possible implication is that she has, early in her life, learnt to attract sympathy by pretence of grief. The Angel, of course, also represents all that Christ stands for, but the Maiden Queen chooses the world of Experience, thinking herself safer there. A conscious and deliberate choice ("I dried my tears & armd my fears") has been made. When the Angel tries a second time (the Second Coming), it is too late: "the time of youth had fled/And grey hairs were on my head." Secrecy ("hid"), shame ("the morn blush'd rosy red"), terror ("fears"), cruelty ("ten thousand shields and spears"), will be her world. If she fails to realise what the dream is telling her she will forfeit joy, love, spontaneity, and ultimately redemption ("he came in vain"). The illustration mimics the figures we see in paintings of Venus and Cupid. The Maiden Queen lies on her right side, facing away from the Cupid-like Angel, her left hand pushing him away or, if you agree with Keynes, "exacting pity from a winged Cupid for her simulated grief". Behind them the morn is blushing rosy red.

**Notes**

[1] It is also possible to read this poem as exhibiting regretful sadness, an awareness of having got things wrong in the past.

[2] Thompson, *Witness against the Beast.*

[3] Shakespeare, as Blake will have known, has a great many references to roses infected with a canker, his favoured adjective for it being "loathsome".

[4] For a fuller discussion see Michael Simpson's essay, Who Didn't Kill Blake's Fly: Moral Law and the Rule of Grammar in '*Songs of Experience*', in *William Blake*, ed. Lucas.

# 10. The forests of the night

## *The Tyger – My Pretty Rose Tree – Ah! Sun-flower – The Lily – The Garden of Love*

Many years ago the BBC broadcast a series of Arts programmes called *Monitor*. One of these was devoted entirely to Blake's *The Tyger*. It collected together responses from a variety of people – children in primary school, a big-game hunter, people in the street, sixth-formers, academics, poets – each of whom had their own take on the poem. Whatever meaning they gave the poem, everyone acknowledged the poem's power and mystery, felt a genuine sense of awe. In most cases their interpretations differed, and yet each of the responses – some confident, some tentative – seemed perfectly plausible. As with the rose and the worm in *The Sick Rose*, the Tyger can accommodate all the meanings we ascribe to it. Meanings radiate from it

*Songs of Innocence* tend to be dynamic in the sense that active communication – even sometimes with things unspoken – takes place, different voices are registered; often (though not always) inverted commas are used; people speak and listen: the shepherd hears the lambs' innocent calls, parents pass on their wisdom, children cannot hold back their enthusiasm, their love. Joy is broadcast and goes on echoing. Sometimes we hear a public voice, sometimes that of the Bard. In *Songs of Experience* on the other hand we tend to be listening to monologues or soliloquies. Dynamic communication is replaced by thought-out statement-making or rhetorical question. Sometimes we are aware of two voices speaking but not interacting. The Clod and the Pebble sing their different songs unaware of each other. The subjects or poems are sometimes apostrophised but given no space in which to reply. Here we meet again the stasis of so many of the poems: question waiting for an answer that doesn't come. The Tyger is addressed but as if from a safe distance. In any case what sort of answers would the Tyger give? If *The Fly* suffers from being cryptic, this same quality is put to service in *The Tyger*. The speaker cannot complete his/her sentences, as if stunned by what is being observed.

*The Tyger* is a another poem of stasis, one that exists solely in the moment of recognition, the held-breath instant the eyes of the hunter and the hunted meet (we may ask who is doing the hunting); it is what we earlier described as the Now of Eternity, the instant between pounce and shot, the same moment the worm injects its poisons – the stasis of question to which no answer is given. All Blake knows is that out there, prowling the universe, is an awesome tigerishness, full of fire and energy, so mighty it is hard to conceive of the Creator who made it and fathom his purpose in doing so. Whatever it is – an incoming intercontinental ballistic missile even – it feels as if it is now on the loose beyond its Maker's control. Is it another aspect of Christ? Christ the Tiger of Eliot's poem 'Gerontion'? Is it the fearful power of a coming revolution? Is it evil or good? Is it both of these together? It certainly has a hypnotic beauty. Was it the same Creator who made the Lamb? Does it epitomise the tigers of wrath, who, in *Proverbs of Hell*, are declared to be "wiser than the horses of instruction"? Is it Lucifer expelled from Heaven? We might remember that Lucifer was once one of God's good angels. Is it his fall that causes the stars to throw down their defences and introduce pity into the universe? His fall, remember, "brought death into the world and all our woes"[1] and brought about the fall of Adam and Eve, causing the earthly paradise, God's Garden of Love, to be replaced by the world of Experience. Well, it is all these things and more.

Tigers appear elsewhere in *Songs*, either as predatory in this world or as caring in the next. "Without contraries is no progression. Attraction and Repulsion, Reason and Energy, Love and Hate, are necessary to Human existence." In some illustrations Blake depicts the Tyger as savage; in the facsimile used here the tiger looks positively cuddly. According to Keynes, this is because Blake "did not intend to dispel the mystery of his poem by painting an animal of consistent and obvious character". This is something we will never be certain of. One thing we can register is that Blake begins by asking how the Tyger's creator "could" fashion such a creature and ends by asking how he "dare". "Could" shows Blake trying to understand it in terms of the kind of labour involved and the kind of space/time continuum it occurred in. "Dare" clearly signals tremendous awe, but is it for the creator or for his creation, or both? It can also imply culpability, allowing the question: how could he let loose such a terrible thing into the universe. One is tempted to read it as a prophecy of nuclear power.

*My Pretty Rose Tree* is sometimes treated as if it depicted an event in Blake's life, a moment of temptation, a knowing look from a beautiful woman, to which he said no-thank-you because he wished to be faithful to Catherine, his wife. This interpretation isn't all that helpful. It is better to think in terms of a generalised narrator and that way accept the truths it expresses as general, universal. Temptation has been put in the speaker's way, and he has turned it down. Even so, guilt has entered his heart like the invisible worm and, being over-attentive to his partner because of his guilt, finds that she – not through knowledge but by instinct – 'knows' something is amiss and turns from him. If guilt and secrecy have entered the speaker's heart, jealousy has entered hers. Both from now on carry infections that isolate them. Blake knew perfectly Christ's words in Matthew 5:28: "whosoever looketh on a woman to lust after her hath committed adultery with her already in his heart." The poem shows how easy it is, unwittingly, to damage a relationship. In a way it is a variation on the story of Adam and Eve – the serpent has entered the garden – but inverting it so that it is the man who is tempted, and ironising it so that he is guilty in thought but not in deed. That said, one of the *Proverbs of Hell* says: "He who desires but acts not, breeds pestilence." Take this into account and the poem takes on other depths. Does the narrator regret passing "the sweet flower o'er"? Another *Proverb* tells us:

"Shame is Pride's cloak." Maybe the narrator, without wanting to, betrays the fact that he has been flattered. Whatever the case, the poem is psychologically extremely astute.

It is engraved on the same plate as *Ah! Sun-flower* and *The Lilly* and is the only one to show any figures. What we see, to the left, is a young man seated and doubled up with grief, to his right a woman reclining on her side, looking positively indifferent, like the female figure in *The Angel* and Earth in *Introduction* and *The Little Girl Found*.

*Ah! Sun-flower* is another jewel of a poem – perfectly crafted. Its rhythms are like those of a funeral march, slow and heavy – three drum-beat stresses to each line. All energy has been sapped away. Again, we are held in a moment of stasis – between rootedness in the earth and heavenward aspiration. It is a poem of yearning. The flower, an emblem of the sun, but also of the desire to be quit of the slings and arrows of this world, gazes longingly skyward to that realm where all is sweetness and light. Unable to follow, the sun-flower watches the "Youth pined away with desire" and the "pale Virgin shrouded in snow" – victims of unfulfilled sexual desire – heading upwards for their consolations and rewards.

It would be wrong, I'm sure, to see this poem as morbidly expressing a death wish. It is in tune with all the other poems that look forward to journeys ending in rest in "the sweet golden clime" of Eternity.

*The Lilly* is the shortest of the *Songs*. The lily – normally an emblem of purity (lilies are associated with the Virgin Mary) but also of death – is compared to the rose with its aggressive thorns and the sheep with its "threatening horn". It would seem to be a symbol of perfection, an emblem of Innocence. If we were tempted to interpret the three poems engraved on the single plate as personal, we might say that after the grief of rejection and the longing to be free of it, Blake's married happiness, celebrated in the lily's delight in Love, has been restored.

Are the modesty of the rose and the humility of the sheep false? Are they saying: 'Keep your distance'? The lily has no need of weapons. Her beauty and her delight in Love are all-sufficient. Is this a case of the "soul of sweet delight [which] can never be defil'd"? Here for once is someone who needs no guardian or protector? But is this too a form of self-deception – the lily proud of her perfection? Other poems in *Songs* would suggest so. And the word "stain" perhaps indicates a stance of *noli me tangere* ("Touch me not").

When he lived in Lambeth Blake's house had a garden in which, according to Peter Ackroyd, he grew marigolds and a vine. Was this his private version of Eden, the "garden mild"?

*The Garden of Love* is of course a garden of vision not a real one. The poem, like *Ah! Sun-flower*, has the rhythms of a march – not so much a funeral march as a quasi-military one – which, in its last two lines, become utterly menacing, their jackboot regularity a form of grinding tyranny. The speaker revisits the site of the Garden of Love (at base the Garden of Eden but also anywhere associated with the innocence of youth) only to find a Chapel, surrounded by graves and hedged in with restrictive thorny briars. Where joy and play might once have been seen on an echoing green, and where flowers once grew, now there is the Temple of Prohibitions ("Thou shalt not, writ over the door"). It is the Church of Satan, the God of the Old Testament. Caterpillars (priests) have eaten up the flowers and filled the place with graves (which Keynes calls "the graves of the instincts"). The priests also, as agents of the moral law, deny freedoms, particularly sexual ("desires") freedom, and they walk their rounds like prison guards. A *Proverb of Hell* states "As the caterpillar chooses the fairest leaves to lay her eggs, so the priest lays his curse on the fairest joys." In the illustration we see two children, heads bowed towards the ground, in a dark place kneeling beside a priest who is indoctrinating them in the repressive religion he serves. It is as if they are not daring to move.

**Notes**
1 Milton, *Paradise Lost*, i.3.

# 11. There grows one in the Human Brain
## The Little Vagabond – London –
## The Human Abstract – Infant Sorrow

If *The Garden of Love* gives us an adult reaction to the Church of the False Religion, *The Little Vagabond* gives us a child's more innocent, and therefore wiser, one. He can see there is a solution. It is a cheery poem with good sing-along rhythm. The child, addressing his mother, speaks with the same certainty as the child in *The Lamb* but this time voicing his feelings about the world of Experience as he perceives it. He knows better than his mother how this world works. If she is in thrall to it, what as a mother can we say of her? He is also talking to Mother Earth and in this sense *The Little Vagabond* parallels *Introduction* to *Songs of Experience*.

The boy's mother is being advised by her son, but we hardly get the feeling she is listening. The lad's experience of the Church is one of unnecessary discomfort, which she obviously accepts as normal: it's too cold, physically and spiritually ("Such usage in heaven will never do well"), whereas the Alehouse (conventionally a place of sin) is a warm and jolly place. It offers conviviality, the human warmth of friendship. It was also, we should remember, where political meetings often took place, where dangerous ideas were voiced. Ale and a pleasant fire, in the vagabond's eyes, would do wonders for the soul, not just satisfy the needs of the body. It would make for singing and happiness and make God so happy that He would no longer have any quarrel with the Devil: He would "kiss him & give him both drink and apparel". From what has been called "the dynamic interplay of opposing forces"[1] Blake is looking to a synthesis in which true wisdom can be found. The child sees prophetically through the eyes as well as physically with them. And to him the solution is simple. A world without antagonisms is possible. Adopt the solution and there'd be no more unhealthy or ill-treated children. Is 'naive' a good word to use of this vision? The boy is idealistic certainly; he is 'naive' only to those who are conditioned by the values of the illusory material world. But his idealism/radicalism can also be seen as a form of dangerous dissidence. Blake wants to awaken the transformative energies of revolution to restore a lost age of innocence. It is not for nothing the poem was omitted from the first typographical edition of 1839.

In the engraved plate, God is seen above the poem blazing with darkness-dispelling light and comforting a youth, while below a couple and their children sit round a fire in attitudes of dejection.

*London* is Blake's grimmest vision of the kingdom of Satan. It is often assumed that Blake is speaking in his own voice about his beloved city, outraged at the social, political and religious injustices of his time. Well, yes, but the illustration shows a youth leading an aged man with a long flowing beard supporting himself on a crutch The lad is almost certainly showing Urizen the horrors he has brought or is bringing into being: it is more likely the boy is the poem's narrator and the poem both an indictment and a record of his vision of hell. It can be read as a warning, a prophecy of what the city is turning into as much as an account of prevailing conditions. To read it as such would give the poem a positive edge and act as a counter to those who see it as cynically pessimistic.

The city is a visionary place, a Babylon, the opposite of the New Jerusalem Blake wants us to build; it is full of faces (not complete human beings) all marked with distress – anticipating Eliot's "unreal city" in which "A crowd flowed over London Bridge, so many,/I had not thought death had undone so many."[2] It is a city ruled by Mammon, commercially carved up ("charter'd")[3], its people imprisoned in the mechanical philosophy Blake blames Newton, Locke, and Hobbes for, which extols Reason above his sacrosanct Imagination, and therefore, because it proceeds from "mind", creating conditions of slavery to the repressive ideologies of Church and State.

According to Kropotkin, "throughout the history of our civilisation two traditions, two opposing tendencies have confronted each other: the Roman and the popular, the imperial and the federalist, the authoritarian and the libertarian."[4] Blake nails his colours to the mast of the latter, knowing it to be Christ's world. He looks forward to the end of empire, calls for sexual and racial equality and freedom, and for universal tolerance. And something we need to recognise: he was not alone nor was he the lone madman some have thought him to be; there were many sects at the time using biblical language to voice their radicalism, similarly calling on Earth to rise "from the slumberous mass" and shake off her chains, her "mind-forged manacles".

London is a city of shame and fear, evidenced in the faces of its inhabitants: the cry of the chimney sweeper brings shame on the "blackning Church", the "hapless" death of the soldier (whose last breath is brilliantly and movingly enacted in the sibilance of "hapless Soldiers sigh") brings shame on the monarchical institution he is required to defend and give his life for. (His sibilant expiring breath, that hapless sigh running in blood down a wall, is for me a moment of absolute poetry, of great art.) But worst for Blake is the corruption and perversion of sexual relationships. Prostitutes, unwanted children (blasting "the new-born Infants tear"), venereal diseases (blighting "with plagues the Marriage hearse") – the city swarming with invisible worms.

If *London* makes us *see* the Kingdom of Satan, *The Human Abstract* (it was at one point called *The Human Image*) spells the argument out for us. 'Abstract' here I'm sure means something separated from matter – in other words the soul. It declares that if the human soul were compounded of the Christ-like virtues, Heaven would be built in Hell's despair. The problem is that the world thrives on antagonisms; we need to invent enemies to help define our identities through opposition. As another *Proverb of Hell* says "The crow wish'd everything was black, the owl that everything was white." Dualistic thinking again: black is black by virtue of the fact that it is the opposite of white. This, seeded in the human brain, "grows" – like the Tyger and the invisible worm, it has a dynamic existence seemingly all its own. Not even the "Gods of the earth and sea" – which I take to mean the cleverest people alive – understand this. In this poem Blake encompasses all of human history: how out of distrust and selfish love comes cruelty, which in turn breeds false humility, which in turn creates the False Religion ("Mystery") fed on by priests and their like ("the Caterpillar and the Fly") and offering, like the Serpent-Satan, the attractive but forbidden fruit from the Tree of Knowledge. The Raven who lives in its branches is Death; its fruit is associated with "Deceit" – in other words this religion is based on lies deliberately cultivated, watered with tears. The illustration shows Urizen tangled in snares of his own (and our) making.

Blake again maintains that abstraction, the processes of reason, is destructive of all we have seen Innocence embodying. He therefore sets Imagination, Vision, the Energy of Impulse and Instinct in opposition to Urizen's Reason. He states in his *Proverbs*: "What is now proved was once only imagin'd" and "Everything possible to be believ'd is an image of truth." If God is to be seen in the human, so too is the Devil. The poem's counterpart in *Innocence* is of course *The Divine Image* in which God and man are seen to be one and all religions equal if they pray to the Human Form Divine which is compounded of Mercy, Pity, Peace and Love. In Geoffrey Keynes' words, it is "a statement of true faith in the divinity of unrepressed human instincts and the holiness of life".

If *Infant Joy* is full of joyous spontaneity, *Infant Sorrow* is a *knowing* poem, one that shows Reason in action. It reveals a wilful consciousness in the I-thought-best of its soliloquist, in the intentionality of "sulk" and "leapt", and in the knowingness of its allusions, both biblical and classical. The suggestiveness of "swaddling bands" and its connection with Christ's Nativity is obvious; "bound and weary" brings Prometheus and Adam ("Adam lay ybounden")[5] to mind. The poem is a powerful manifesto of a delinquent plotting to take on the world, turning his seeming weaknesses – helplessness, nakedness, piping loud

– into awesome weapons. In Northrop Frye's words, he is "a little bundle of anarchic will, whose desires take no account of either the social or natural order".[6] In *Infant Sorrow* we hear the cerebral click of mental cogs as the child's brain forms its tactical decision, in what is for my money one of the most awesome enjambements in English poetry:

> I thought best
> To sulk ...

This is not submission or defeat but rather a tactical biding of time. This child is a ticking time bomb. What an absolute word 'sulk' is! Try putting another word in its place.

Given that the poem is a soliloquy, we might expect to see a lone-figure illustration. In fact what we are shown is an angry-faced woman attempting to lift a child dodging away (it looks as though he is calling on or wishing to fly up to Heaven) from her extended arms. The scene is a claustrophobic room with the infant's bed set before the parental bed draped with heavy green curtains. It is a scene of oppression.

To all intents and purposes, this is a poem about a child born directly into the world of Experience. He is immediately associated with sorrow and resentment. His birth causes his mother to groan and his father to weep. We have a portrait of a child marked for life. His reaction is to plan revenge. He is the potential delinquent. He may also be, as Christ the Tiger, the spirit of revolution.

**Notes**
[1] Marshall, *Blake, Visionary Anarchist*.
[2] Eliot, *The Waste Land*
[3] There is a possible irony in the fact that charters are often documents determining certain freedoms.
[4] Quoted by Marshall in *Blake, Visionary Anarchist*.
[5] A 15th-century anonymous carol.
[6] Northrop Frye, "Blake's Treatment of the Archetype" in *English Romantic Poets: Modern Essays in Criticism*, ed. M.H. Abrams (Oxford University Press, 1956).

# 12. Are such things done on Albions shore?

## *A Poison Tree – A Little Boy Lost –*
## *A Little Girl Lost*

Blake's poems are psychologically wise. *A Poison Tree* is a case in point. Long before Freud, he grasped the destructive power of repressed psychic energies. When the narrator of *A Poison Tree* tells us he didn't bottle up the anger he felt towards a friend but openly expressed it, he knew he would be freed of its ill-effects; he also knew from his Bible that you should never let the sun go down upon your wrath (Ephesians 4:26). But he also understood that repressed emotion not only distorts a person's life but can actually be used maliciously:

> I was angry with my foe;
> I told it not, my wrath did grow.

Like the invisible worm and the tiger, the wrath takes on a life of its own. But the narrator deliberately cultivates, almost lovingly tends it – and here again it is mind that is doing all the damage. Ironically, the foe is of the same cast of mind: "And he *knew* that it was mine" (my italics). One of the *Proverbs of Hell* states: "He who has suffer'd you to impose on him, knows you."

The scene re-enacts once more the moment in the Garden of Eden – the narrator playing a satanic role that causes the foe to eat of the apple and find death in it. He has done the Devil's work, has broken the golden rule of loving one's neighbour, and insulted Christ's doctrine of forgiveness. He does not let the sun go down upon his wrath. The poem itself, like so many others, dynamically enacts a process of growth and demonstrates Blake's fine dramatic skills. The friction between contraries generates energy. There are, for one thing, seven 'ands' at work pushing the poem onward. The second line of the last verse is tactically superb: it acts as a kind of hushed moment – like the gap between the two stanzas of *The Sick Rose* – before the delivery of the punch in the final two:

> And into my garden stole,
> When the night had veild the pole;
> In the morning glad I see,
> My foe outstretchd beneath the tree.

The illustration shows the foe's dead body flat on its back, head towards us, arms outstretched in an attitude of crucifixion.

*A Little Boy Lost* too has an unrelenting pulse that races towards a fearful climax. As in *The Little Vagabond*, the boy relates what he sees and understands, from experience, of the world he inhabits. There is no irony in his plea; there are only statements based upon experience. The first part of the poem is a prayer addressed to God the Father. But God in the boy's experience only offers subsistence-level crumbs. His world is the upside-down one of selfish love. This is the wrong God of state religion. A priest, overhearing the boy's prayer, immediately pounces on it and denounces it as heretical. The boy becomes a martyr for the truth that a repressive patriarchal society cannot bear to listen to. And this time the parents, in agonies of grief, are victims too.

The poem is full of active ironies. The "Father" turns out to be the evil God of selfishness and reason; his priest is alive with energy ("trembling zeal") directed towards perverse ends; he denounces the boy as a "fiend" to an admiring populace; and describes the religion he serves as "most holy". Perhaps the heaviest irony lies in the fact that the child is accused of setting reason up, the very thing that creates mind-forged manacles. So he is burned in a holy place, where "many had been burn'd before" – which reminds us there have been many precedents in the fate of witches and so-called heretics in previous ages. So the last line's question is rhetorical: does this really still go on in the Age of Enlightenment in England?

The burning at the stake is a symbol for whatever is done to Innocence by way of corrupting, exploiting, enslaving, and destroying it. The poem is an expression of *saeva indignatio* (fierce outrage) but it is not just an indictment, it is also, like *The Dream,* an *in extremis* wake-up call. The illustration shows the child's parents kneeling in abject grief in front of flames. To the right, ivy, which Keynes describes as a symbol of vengeance, swirls upwards. The Bible has this to tell us (and this applies as much to the previous poem):

> Dearly beloved, avenge not yourselves, but rather give place unto wrath. Vengeance is mine; I will repay, saith the Lord. Therefore if thine enemy hunger, feed him; if he thirst, give him drink: for in doing so thou shalt heap coals of fire on his head. Be not overcome of evil, but overcome evil with good. Romans 12: 19-21

*A Little Girl Lost* addresses the future. The prophet/bard relates a story/parable prefaced by four lines in which he unequivocally states his indignation at the way Love is understood and treated in his time, and confidently declares that future ages are going to find this hard to understand. The implication is that good will one day triumph: out of the struggle between polarised energies will come what Peter Marshall calls "the higher synthesis of Divine Humanity". This kind of thinking and feeling re-emerged in the mid-twentieth century and Blake was honoured among many young people as a contemporary. The American poet Allen Ginsberg[1] was central and his influence spread through the Liverpool poets into poetry generally. In 1969 Penguin brought out an anthology edited by Michael Horovitz entitled *Children of Albion: Poetry of the 'Underground' in Britain.* Horovitz made this claim in the *Afterwords*:

In songs of innocence & experience to the calculated threats to contemporary life as Blake's were – catching up and redirecting rays from the talented maker of underground movies and posters and music and environments – we're cleansing language of the perversions wished upon it by Admass 'brainwashers', ghost writers, statesmen of all nations ... The unfinished work of Blake is ours to carry on. The legacy of the whole man.

Most of these feelings have now sunk back into the 'Underground' – though Blake's challenges may be said to be just as imperative as they ever were.

Though the story the prophet/bard tells is one involving sexual love[2], Blake wants us to think of Love in all its manifestations, which find their summation in Christ. And somewhere in all of this he almost certainly wants us to remember the story of Onan in Genesis killed by Jehovah for *coitus interruptus*. Onan gave his name to onanism which is generally descriptive of any form of sexual self-gratification. Commentators have suggested other associations. Using the name 'Ona' may be something similar to D.H. Lawrence's vain wish to cleanse sexual language of its accrued dirtiness.

The prophet describes an Age of Gold when nakedness was no sin – prelapsarian Adam and Eve delighting in the sunny beams of "holy light". Against this background, a pair of lovers, with noone around, is found playing in the beams of this same holy light. They agree to go back at night-time, to re-enact the Fall, suggesting that they will have sex in secret, or possibly elope (it is clear that Blake imagines the Fall is played out over and over in people's lives). But when Ona appears before her father (Jehovah-like with his "hoary hair") he instinctively knows what she's been up to, however innocent it may be, and expresses his concern. She has entered or is about to enter into womanhood, but her brightness ("the maiden bright") is swept aside by his "loving look" and "holy book" doubtless open at the Old Testament.

His love for her, like the invisible worm's for the rose, is possessive. She enters Experience infected by her father's fears ("All her tender limbs with terror shook"). The innocent love she has experienced with her lover is now damaged. In the sky depicted in the illustration birds, as in so many of the engravings, are seen flying, symbols of freedom from restraint.

**Notes**

[1] Ginsberg declared that Blake came in a vision and sang his *Songs* to him.

[2] For a fascinating account of the importance of sex to Blake read *Why Mrs Blake Cried: William Blake and the Sexual Basis of Spiritual Vision* by Marsha Keith Schuchard (Century 2006).

# 13. Image of truth new born
## To Tirzah – The School-Boy –
## The Voice of the Ancient Bard – A Divine Image

In 1 Corinthians 15:44, St Paul writes of the existence of two bodies, the natural and the spiritual: "It is sown a natural body; it is raised a spiritual body. There is a natural body, and there is a spiritual body." Blake quotes words from this verse adding them as a tag to *To Tirzah,* a late inclusion into *Songs.* He also incorporates some of them into the illustration.

Nature to Blake was not the external physical world perceived by the senses (hence his quarrel with Wordsworth)[1] but, as we have stated, rather what existed in and through the imagination. It is worth quoting at length from the letter Blake wrote to a Dr Trusler on 23rd August 1799:

> I feel that a man may be happy in This World. And I know that This World is a world of Imagination and Vision. I see Everything I paint in This World, but Every body does not see alike. To the Eyes of a Miser a Guinea is far more beautiful than the Sun, & a bag worn with use of Money has more beautiful proportions than a Vine filled with Grapes. The tree which moves some to tears is in the Eyes of others only a Green thing which stands in the way. Some see Nature all Ridicule & Deformity, & by these I shall not regulate my proportions; & and some scarce see Nature at all. But to the Man of Imagination, Nature is Imagination itself. As a man is, so he sees. As the Eye is formed, such are its Powers. You certainly Mistake, when you say that Visions of Fancy are

not to be found in This World. To Me This World is all One continued vision of Fancy or Imagination, & I feel Flatter'd when I am told so. What is it sets Homer, Virgil & Milton in so high a rank of Art? Why is the Bible more entertaining & instructive than any other book? Is it not because they are addressed to the Imagination, which is Spiritual sensation, & but mediately to the Understanding & Reason? Such is true painting, and such was alone valued by the Greeks & the best modern Artists.

Given the above, it is wrong for us to look for meanings to Blake's poems in what he calls, somewhat disparagingly, This World – in what we might call reality.

*To Tirzah* puts motherly love and sexual love into the perspective and context of Eternity, daringly quoting Christ's words, not once but twice, those spoken to his mother at the marriage at Cana of Galilee and recorded in John 2:1–4. The words of the poem, however, are addressed to Tirzah, a name casually mentioned in the Song of Solomon 6:4[2] where she seems to suggest sexual desire. (*Verse 5* urges the beloved to "Turn away thine eyes from me, for they have overcome me").

If *A Little Girl Lost* warns against patriarchal possessiveness, *To Tirzah* warns against its matriarchal form ("Thou Mother of my Mortal part"). But of course Blake does not simply mean a birth-mother but Eve, the mother of us all, and ultimately Earth herself. Being born on the Earth means, as Buddhists insist, enduring suffering; it means having to cope with the consequences of the Fall, the separation of the sexes; it means work and sorrow. The archetypal mother of the poem is made responsible for all of this – and it is all stated factually.

Given a proper perspective, the speaker is able to rejoice in what he/she has known all along, that "Mercy changd Death into Sleep" and "The Death of Jesus set me free": the ultimate freedom is from Nature as perceived by the senses into the realm of Imagination and Vision where the spirit is liberated from the bonds of physical being, the cycle Eliot describes as 'birth, copulation and death'. "One short sleep past," wrote Donne, "we wake eternally" That being the case, the speaker of the poem is not so much high-mindedly rejecting as confidently looking forward to a promised freedom.

The illustration shows two women attempting to hold up the natural body of a distressed (dead?) man, whilst a white-bearded figure pours water from a jug over him. The women, according to Keynes, represent "'Mother-love and Sex-love, who have failed to save him." The aged figure is offering him the water of life.

*The School-Boy* was originally included in *Songs of Innocence* and indeed it would sit better there than coming after the poems we have been most recently discussing. Good poem though it undoubtedly is, it doesn't extend any of the thoughts or feelings we have been encountering but simply reconnects us with the contraries of joy and restraint. We can only speculate on Blake's wishes in placing it here – maybe to lighten the tone before signing off with his final poem *The Voice of the Ancient Bard*. Not that it is a light-hearted poem. School, like the little vagabond's Church, is being used as a symbol of deadly constraint, another example of mind-forged manacles. It asks questions about what sort of future we are preparing ourselves for and, in this way, connects with the poem that follows it. And it asks these questions of parents who, we may infer, are being accused for their part in creating the conditions the boy complains of. The poem should not be read as anti-education but anti the wrong kind of education, one that is an extension of state control and fails to recognise creative energy. Swinburne said of Blake: "To serve art and love liberty seemed to him two things (if indeed they were not one thing) worth a man's life and work,"[3]

In the illustration the poem is encircled with vines which boys climb up (one is already at the top reading a book); on the ground there are three in kneeling or seated positions, perhaps gathering the fruits.

*The Voice of the Ancient Bard* is not, in my view, the most successful poem to end on. To my mind it changes direction halfway through. Like *The School-Boy* it was originally meant for *Songs of Innocence*. Because the Bard is 'ancient', he represents the transcendent truth of all the ages: he can, as the opening stanza of *Introduction* tells us, see "Present, Past, & Future". Here he celebrates with "Youth of delight" the dawn of a new age and the dispersal of the clouds of doubt and reason. We think we are emerging from *Experience* on a positive note. But then the bard takes on an admonitory tone and becomes more like Virgil revealing to Dante the conditions of Hell. It is as if the Bard is obsessed by the infernal vision of the world of Experience, so that what started on an upbeat turns cloudy. It is noticeable that the rhythm in the last three lines changes awkwardly – though this might be defended as re-enacting the stumbling steps being taken. There is also a conflict of tenses, in that if we are present at the new dawn, why are the stumbling blind continuing to lead the blind? Is this Christ's separation of sheep and goats as promised in Matthew 25?

*The Voice of the Ancient Bard* has every feeling of being a draft. The illustration straightforwardly shows a white-bearded Bard with a harp singing to a gathering of young people.

There is finally the matter of the uncoloured engraving showing Los (symbol of the craftsman) hammering the poem *A Divine Image* into shape added to the Oxford/Trianon edition as a supplementary plate. It is said to show "the extreme violence of Blake's feelings", perhaps as a reaction to the war with France. Well perhaps, though that kind of comment can only be speculative.

*A Divine Image* has, however, its counterpart in *Innocence* in *The Divine Image* and fits perfectly well with the expression of Blake's ideas as we have been discussing them. The choice of definite and indefinite articles is the key. *The* Divine Image is one of incontrovertible truth belonging to Eternity; *a* Divine Image is the illusory one belonging to *Experience*. Mercy, Pity, Peace and Love are turned on their heads to become Cruelty, Jealousy, Terror and Secrecy. If the Kingdom of God is within, so is the province of Urizen. "All deities", said

Blake "reside in the human breast." And again, "He who sees the Infinite in all things sees God. He who sees the Ratio sees only himself. Therefore God becomes as we are, that we may be as he is."

What is needed is to reconcile energy, reason, emotion and spirit by progressing through what Blake called fourfold vision.[4] To risk putting this complex matter in simple terms: Man has four levels of consciousness to pass through if he is to see "everything as it is, Infinite". Single vision ("Newton's sleep") is a state of darkness where Reason holds sway; twofold is all fire and energy, the level experienced by the creative artist and the lover; threefold is when light unites fire and energy, Heaven and Hell (it is here sexual love can give a glimpse of full vision); fourfold vision is the spirit in a state of full light in which all contraries are reconciled. In the poem *To Thomas Butts* Blake wrote

> Now I a fourfold vision see,
> And a fourfold vision is given to me;
> 'Tis fourfold in my supreme delight,
> And threefold in soft Beulah's night,
> And twofold always. – May God us keep
> From single vision, and Newton's sleep!

(Beulah = married. To Blake it means the threshold of Eternity, a state of soul in which Contraries are all equally true, and there is complete sexual fulfilment).

*A Divine Image* may be thought of by some as an expression of an anger Blake did not wish to expose in *Songs*. But had we found it located halfway-through *Songs of Experience* I doubt we'd be taken aback by it. Los, in the engraving, is not so much Blake but the archetypal artist.

"I will not", Blake wrote, "Reason & Compare: my business is to Create."

## Notes

[1] Of Wordsworth Blake wrote "I see in Wordsworth the Natural Man rising up against the Spiritual Man Continually, & then he is No Poet, but a Heathen Philosopher at Enmity against all true Poetry or Inspiration ... Natural Objects did & and now do weaken, deaden and obliterate Imagination in Me. Wordsworth must know that what he writes Valuable is not to be found in Nature."

[2] "Thou art beautiful, o my love, as Tirzah, comely as Jerusalem, terrible as an army with banners."

[3] *William Blake: A Critical Essay* (1868) (Folcraft Library, 1977).

[4] For an account of this see Beer, *Blake's Humanism*.

# GREENWICH EXCHANGE BOOKS

# STUDENT GUIDE LITERARY SERIES

The Greenwich Exchange Student Guide Literary Series is a collection of essays on major or contemporary serious writers in English and selected European languages. The series is for the student, the teacher and 'common readers' and is an ideal resource for libraries. The *Times Educational Supplement* praised these books, saying, "The style of [this series] has a pressure of meaning behind it. Readers should learn from that ... If art is about selection, perception and taste, then this is it."

(ISBN prefix 978-1-871551 applies unless marked*, when the prefix 978-1-906075 applies.

The series includes:
**Antonin Artaud** by Lee Jamieson (98-3)
**W.H. Auden** by Stephen Wade (36-5)
**Honoré de Balzac** by Wendy Mercer (48-8)
**William Blake** by Peter Davies (27-3)
**The Brontës** by Peter Davies (24-2)
**Robert Browning** by John Lucas (59-4)
**Lord Byron** by Andrew Keanie (83-9)
**Samuel Taylor Coleridge** by Andrew Keanie (64-8)
**Joseph Conrad** by Martin Seymour-Smith (18-1)
**William Cowper** by Michael Thorn (25-9)
**Charles Dickens** by Robert Giddings (26-9)
**Emily Dickinson** by Marnie Pomeroy (68-6)
**John Donne** by Sean Haldane (23-5)
**Ford Madox Ford** by Anthony Fowles (63-1)
**The Stagecraft of Brian Friel** by David Grant (74-7)
**Robert Frost** by Warren Hope (70-9)
**Patrick Hamilton** by John Harding (99-0)
**Thomas Hardy** by Sean Haldane (33-4)
**Seamus Heaney** by Warren Hope (37-2)
**Joseph Heller** by Anthony Fowles (84-6)
**Gerard Manley Hopkins** by Sean Sheehan (77-3)
**James Joyce** by Michael Murphy (73-0)